The Coffee Shop Business Plan

How to Open a Coffee Shop and Ensure It's Successful, Popular, and Profitable

by Jonathan Schafer

Table of Contents

Introduction 1

Chapter 1: The Big Mistake 7

Chapter 2: The Best Location 13

Chapter 3: The Best Product 17

Chapter 4: The Best Process 23

Chapter 5: The Best Service 27

Chapter 6: The Best Plan 33

Conclusion 37

Introduction

I've written this book to provide prospective entrepreneurs a guide to opening and managing a coffee shop new business. Coffee shops are one of those businesses people assume are simple and easy to run. With major brand coffee dispensaries popping up on nearly every block of big cities, many assume that it can't be too hard to run a profitable independent location.

They'd be wrong.

The vast majority of cafes actually fail. That failure is not necessarily bankruptcy, though. More often, it is the slow loss of time and savings to keep the business operating. Such coffee shops drain capital from investors and deflate the dreams of those who start them. But it doesn't have to be this way.

I wrote this book to provide you with a simple series of steps to make sure you succeed where others fail. If you have dreamed of owning your own coffee shop and saved money from working a regular nine to five gig, this is more than just a business venture. It's a chance to create something.

If you're like me, you've spent long hours at a boring and unfulfilling job, and now you want to do something worthwhile with the rest of your life. And why not a coffee shop? After all, selling coffee should be easy. It's a legal, addictive stimulant that many people need, want, and love. How hard can it be to succeed?

That simplistic view ignores the many circumstances that make or break coffee shops. In the coming pages, I will lay out each of these factors as well as the common traps novice proprietors fall into. This book will show you what you need to do to succeed.

© Copyright 2014 by LCPublifish LLC - All rights reserved.

This document is geared towards providing reliable information in regards to the topic and issue covered. The publication is sold with the idea that the publisher is not required to render accounting, officially permitted, or otherwise, qualified services. If advice is necessary, legal or professional, a practiced individual in the profession should be ordered.

- From a Declaration of Principles which was accepted and approved equally by a Committee of the American Bar Association and a Committee of Publishers and Associations.

In no way is it legal to reproduce, duplicate, or transmit any part of this document in either electronic means or in printed format. Recording of this publication is strictly prohibited and any storage of this document is not allowed unless with written permission from the publisher. All rights reserved.

The information provided herein is stated to be truthful and consistent, in that any liability, in terms of inattention or otherwise, by any usage or abuse of any policies, processes, or directions contained within is solely and completely the responsibility of the recipient reader. Under no circumstances will any legal responsibility or blame be held against the publisher for any reparation, damages, or monetary loss due to the information herein, either directly or indirectly.

Respective authors own all copyrights not held by the publisher.

The information herein is offered for informational purposes solely, and is universal as so. The presentation of the information is without contract or any type of guarantee assurance.

The trademarks that are used are without any consent, and the publication of the trademark is without permission or backing by the trademark owner. All trademarks and brands within this book are for clarifying purposes only and are the owned by the owners themselves, not affiliated with this document.

Chapter 1: The Big Mistake

Rather than just present a plan for success, I wanted to warn you of the mistakes that new owners commonly make to start. I typically give this advice to everyone who asks me about starting their own business, no matter the venture. You'll see me repeat it throughout the book. "Never let the perfect become the enemy of the best." (That's a derivation from Voltaire)

What do I mean? We aspire to the ideal of perfection. Whether we want to acknowledge that is irrelevant. How many new proprietors have been held captive by this kind of thinking on opening day of their café? They want everything to be perfect. The chairs must be perfectly comfortable. The coffee must be perfectly brewed. The pastries and snacks must be perfectly delicious.

Even though their openings are great success, they fail to achieve their idealistic vision. Nothing will ever be perfect. The only thing that is perfect on opening day were their expectations. They were perfectly out of line with reality.

Let's stay reality-based together. I want you to shoot for your best not for what you believe would be perfect at this moment. Attaining your best factors in all the things outside your span of control. That makes it a realistic endeavor and not a never-ending quest for something always just a little out of reach.

When new business owners want things to be perfect, they seek to avoid any perceived failure at all costs. With any business, a certain amount of imperfection or failure can and should be tolerated. That might seem like unusual advice, but it is undeniably true. To succeed in any venture, but especially in owning a coffee shop, the first lesson you must internalize is that you are allowed to fail.

Most people cling to that old movie line, "Failure is not an option." While none of us want to fail, sometimes a mistake is just what we need to propel our business to greater success. Failure isn't the end of the world. In fact, I subscribe to the theory that failure is really just a lesson in how to succeed. How well you learn from your initial missteps will determine the likelihood of your long term success.

When people fear mistakes, they exert additional effort to make sure everything is exactly perfect. The problem that they refuse to accept is that nothing is perfect. In striving for perfection we fail to understand how to truly succeed.

This business is one where failure occurs daily. Consider your display case filled with delectable treats that accompany the coffee. Most every night you'll discard the large quantities of product. Our instinctual response is to look at that waste as a sign of failure.

The next day a new owner will be tempted to put less in the case fearful another full bag of wasted pastries. Many owners will also keep product a little longer hoping someone will buy it.

While that makes plenty of objective sense, a sparsely populated display case tells customers that the coffee shop is skimping, which creates the perception of poor quality. As does the first bite of product past its prime window of consumption. Instead of reducing waste, the owner has instead alienated customers. Trying to prevent failure only led to more of it.

The successful coffee shop owner won't fixate on minimizing waste. I know of one owner who set up a partnership with a local dairy to trade leftovers from the display case for a lower rate on milk and cream. The farmer used the left over product as supplemental feed. Accepting failure created an opportunity for reduced costs and greater margins. That kind of counterintuitive thinking fosters greater success.

Accepting and embracing mistakes and imperfections not only allows you to correct them, but they help to shape your business. The first business plan you create for a coffee shop is fantastic. I'm emphasizing the element of fantasy in fantastic, because you don't yet know half of what you need to know to make this business work. That's okay. Few people understand what they want to do, without first seeing all the things they do not want to do.

When you are first beginning you don't know what you don't know about this business. Those unknown unknowns are like traps hidden in a green field. If you charge ahead heedlessly you'll spring a trap. Maybe that trap is a mild setback. That's the most common trap. In the aggregate mild setbacks can create major problems.

Sometimes you will encounter a major problem that you had not taken into account when you drew up your business plan. Keeping an open mind to the value of failure in your business will enable you to adapt and correct your course. In doing so, you will have avoided making the big mistake.

Furthermore, adopting the mindset that imperfection and failure are okay will help you from feeling so defeated when you stumble. You'll instead be more resilient, and be able to keep charging forward, knowing that failure is a part of success.

Chapter 2: The Best Location

Many consultants will advise prospective startup coffee shops to focus their attention on picking the "perfect location". They suggest you locate your venture in a high traffic location in a densely populated urban area. There are several downsides to this proposition. Rents are high. The congestion forces many people to hurry by rather than stop. Competition is also highest in these areas.

Instead of seeking the "perfect" location, I want you to focus on attaining a "goldilocks scenario". Rather than perfect, it needs to be just right. There are no perfect locations. But there are many "just right" locations. A just right location will have consistent traffic, reasonable population density, complementary rather than competitive neighbors and the best possible cost of occupancy.

What constitutes the just right amount of consistent traffic? Coffee shops need two types of traffic, destination customers and spontaneous customers. Typically, destination customers will cover operating costs and spontaneous customers are what make the café profitable. Weekday traffic patterns are fairly consistent and allow the steady stream of regular clientele. Weekend traffic can be wildly inconsistent. The goldilocks location is a location that has close access to offices and commercial spaces as well as tourist attractions. The traffic doesn't need to be

Times Square, just consistent and somewhat predictable.

When seeking just right amount of population density, look not just for the most people per square mile. Consider the demographics of the area. An upscale café offering artisanal coffee roasts will do just fine in an affluent community populated with young singles. This same coffee shop will have less success in a lower-middle class area, even if the population density is the exact same. The secret to population density is not how many people, but how many of the people I want to attract to my business are in this area.

Neighboring businesses can help funnel the traffic they draw into your store, or they can compete for the existing traffic. The best location will have a mix of non-competitive businesses that cater to the same clientele you seek to have in your store. Using the upscale, artisanal coffee roaster example again, complementary businesses will include boutiques and clothiers that appeal to upmarket consumers. Try to avoid areas saturated with other food options, even if they are not specifically coffee shops.

I once worked in a building in a fairly densely packed part of town filled with offices and businesses that catered to offices. While it was a great, central location, it was a horrible spot for a new coffee shop. The space was inundated with competitors. Not direct competition, like other cafes, but instead quick service restaurants that vie for the same daytime dollars as you will. Sometimes coffee is a complementary acquisition, but for office workers hurrying back to their desks, making a second stop takes up too much time. That made this location a non-starter.

Factoring in this advice should have already created a better result for your rent. By avoiding the location that is perceived as perfect, you also avoid the high cost a landlord wants to charge for the perfect spot. The goal is to spot and capitalize on market inefficiencies. If all retailers are looking for one formula, that will drive up the cost of rent in places that fit their formula. Checking your business' needs against the "perfect" location will open up better opportunities.

Finally, when choosing a location, take to heart the old carpenter's maxim: Measure twice, cut once. No decision is more permanent to your business than the location you select. To the best of your ability, you have to examine, investigate and vet a potential locale before settling on it. Let me offer up one practical piece of advice. When you think you have found your location, bring a few friends who have no experience running a coffee shop and little familiarity with your plans to that location and talk with them about your vision. How quickly they grasp your vision can tell you how well you have picked the spot to help you realize your dream.

Chapter 3: The Best Product

We've shattered all illusions associated with perfection by now, so I'll linger on that topic only briefly to say that when dealing with an agricultural product you will have inconsistencies. Perfection is absolutely impossible. What is possible is finding a superior offering than what you competition is providing. This alone will compensate for every other element of the business plan that falls short.

Espresso beverages are the stars of the coffee shop. Not only are they a creative outlet for the coffee artisans you've hired, they are also the highest margin item on your menu. Getting these right requires devotion to quality both in the sourcing of the beans and also in their preparation. Since preparation is part of the process of making coffee, we'll save that for the next chapter. That leaves the beans themselves. And when you are looking for a single thing that will distinguish your coffee shop, the taste and quality of your coffee is king.

I recall reading one business plan for a café that spent 16 pages detailing everything about their mission except how they were going to source the beans. Ugh. What a waste! How do you blather on around your mission and vision and not go into some level of detail about how you will ensure that your product is in fact the best tasting coffee and espresso?

In fairness, they briefly mentioned that baristas would be trained to properly prepare the coffee. But any coffee connoisseur will correctly point out, if you start with bad beans, you'll get a bad brew. So sourcing superior beans is critical to getting the best possible product.

There are simple rules for getting superior coffee results. The first is obvious, partner with a good roaster. Most coffee shops bring in beans already roasted. If you are going to make this entirely reasonable decision, you need to work with the best possible roaster in your community. Local counts more than you would expect. The freshness of the roast depends largely on the aroma producing acids and oils in roasted beans. For darker roasts, freshness is more critical because much of those oils and acids have been roasted out to create the deep dark browns and blacks of typical espresso roasts.

Secondly, the beans must arrive at the store whole and be ground on site, just before preparation. The grind of the beans contributes to product quality as well. For espresso drinks, the grind must be very fine. To keep your coffee strong and robust you will need a burr grinder, configured for the finest espresso grind. Larger grounds of coffee, which are fine in your average home drip brewed coffee maker will produce weak, flavorless shots of espresso. And you will have alienated customers immediately.

The next item that must be right to produce consistently quality coffee is the machine itself.

Adhering to the rule we established early on, you do not need a perfect espresso machine. Depending on how you lay out your workstations, you may be able to accommodate just one espresso machine. And I would certainly encourage you to open with just one and adjust as demand requires it. Stick with a machine that has at most two group heads.

Your best bet for a new café is a fully automatic or super automatic espresso machine. The fully automatic will regulate both water temperature and pressure as it passes through the espresso. Super automatic machines will handle all that fully automatic machines do, plus grind and tamp the beans. If high volume sales of espresso drinks is part of your growth strategy, paying extra for the super automatic may be a good investment. Keep in mind, bells and whistles are worthless if the coffee produced is undrinkable.

No amount of rewards cards, comfortable chairs, free Wi-Fi or cool ambience will repair a customer relationship that begins with bad coffee. That means devotion to the beans, the grind and the machine is essential. If you go the super automatic route, you will keep the product consistent. One caveat, even though the beans will be ground and tamped, as the proprietor you will still need to master the art of the grind and the tamp.

Before we move on to the process, let me caution you about the one big product mistake many new owners make. They focus so intently on getting product right that they invest more on the prep than they do on the store. Good coffee will overcome nearly everything you do poorly, even an unpleasant store design. Find a balance to begin and upgrade your equipment as you go.

Chapter 4: The Best Process

Process is both the way the coffee is made, but also the way the work areas are laid out to maximize efficiency and productivity. A successful business process involves managing the art of producing perfect pulls of espresso and also understanding the correct means of laying our work stations. Giving employees the necessary training, structure and support will enable them to thrive and serve as brand ambassadors for your coffee shop.

We'll begin with the slowly dying arts of the grind and the tamp. With super automatics beginning to dominate the industry, few baristas and even fewer owners continue to individually grind and tamp their beans. I won't say you must learn these skills. I will tell you that knowing how to prepare espresso without automation allows the thoughtful owner to understand what might be wrong with the expensive equipment that is producing inadequate coffee. The level to which you and your staff can diagnose problems will contribute to providing superior product and service to your customers. And that fosters fierce loyalty.

If you are providing a superior product, your customers will either begin as or gradually become coffee aficionados. They appreciate the attention of someone who understands the process of making coffee and who shares their passion. Your devotion to the art is part of the process of attracting customers and converting them into brand ambassadors.

As much as you want to focus your efforts on maximizing your customer's experience, a successful owner will also ensure that employees can easily and efficiently do their jobs. One area to emphasize is the layout of the store and employee's work areas.

Hospitality businesses cater to people having rough days. They are an oasis of peace in a chaotic world. Have they had a rough day at the office? They'll get some coffee. Are they looking to meet a new client and hold a quick meeting in a casual environment? Coffee shops will facilitate that, too. Are they running behind and need to get a pick me up? That's what coffee was born to do.

What your customers universally want is their product delivered quickly and with a smile. Your team can only do that if you have put effort into designing the store to make their jobs easier. The register area needs to be setup to quickly process transactions and move customers either to the bar where they will wait for their espresso drinks or to the seating area.

The coffee making area needs to be laid out thoughtfully to allow quick and efficient beverage creation. Too much movement does not create the impression of a bustling café. It adds unwanted stress to your employees' days. Their stress shows up in poor service. They are either taking too long to get the orders prepared and delivered, or their frustration is showing up as unintentional frowns on their faces as they deliver the goods.

The best means of combatting that is to keep baristas mostly stationary during beverage preparation. If they don't need to take any steps, they are working smoothly and efficiently. It also means they aren't trying to get by someone who is right next to them. Give the barista access to everything he or she needs: beans, milk, cups, spices, a small clean up sink with hot water, whatever is needed to make the drinks within easy reach. Keep the register near the beverage station. This limits the lost-in-translation effect of orders being shouted across a coffee shop. Doing this will improve efficiency.

Another efficiency innovation is advance prep of as many items as can be done without sacrificing quality. No one wants to walk into a store, order a latte and receive it immediately from a drink warmer. But for pastries and other baked goods, using efficient mass production methods at regular intervals will make sure the goods are fresh and ready when customers want them. Same thing with fresh brewed coffee. Keep it fresh, but make plenty in advance of your peak times. Save the espresso drink making for the moment it is ordered.

.

Chapter 5: The Best Service

Every time a person walks in that door they are offering you the opportunity to serve them for life. The best service you can provide is a superior product. And that will often draw an intense following all by itself. The second most important thing any coffee shop proprietor can do is make it easy to visit.

I recall one such shop that absolutely understood how to make it easy to visit. In a town with half a dozen chain coffee houses, this independent location consistently made money. They knew what it took to make it easy to visit. It was centrally located in a picturesque downtown of a sleepy beach community. It was a frequent destination for townies as well as the seasonal visitors. It had good parking so that the people who worked in the business park on down Main Street could visit and collect their favorite drinks on a break.

The appearance of the store attracted customers, as did their clever name, where the "O" was replaced with a coffee bean. Inside was cozy, which served two purposes. It encouraged people who were in a hurry to come in, get their drink and head out. It gave the other customers a cool place to hang out, meet friends and enjoy themselves while having a cup.

This store understood the lifetime value of a customer. They created weekday specials and leveraged partnerships with local businesses to encourage customers to return. They employed surveys not only to solicit feedback from customers, but to bring customers back again and again.

I'd like to tell you that you only need to make great coffee to ensure frequent patronage. As much as that helps, you need a hook that keeps people coming back. The first and most obvious one is a friendly staff. One shop I frequented had a true genius in their employ. He understood how to balance flavors brilliantly and created handcrafted beverages that his customers came back for. But his skill was not an inborn gift. It was something he learned through trial and error and most importantly by engaging the customers to ask what they liked.

When I met the owner I asked how she had lucked upon such an employee. She told me that her goal in hiring her team was to give them the ability to be themselves. They didn't have to conform to what she thought was best. As long as their customers liked the service they received, she made it clear the team would be rewarded. She empowered her team and her team ran with it.

Service is not just getting them in the door, time and again. It is more frequently about the little touches. Busy coffee shops have lines. Just like every other popular destination. The best service you can provide a customer who has been standing in line is a smile and ease of payment. Coffee is high enough margin that accepting any common credit card will not erode margins. Likewise, offering more modern options such as PayPal, RFID credit card payments and payments off mobile devices will give your customers plenty of options.

One of the best laid out stores I ever visited focused attention to the register and drink bar. The entrances led right past the seating area. As a result most customers would get their drink and snack and look over at the seating area before leaving. The owner had done something very clever that I complimented him on. He had made the seating area seem like the kids table at a family dinner. Out of the way, isolated and where the cool kids would never sit. The few people who did sit there used the space to conduct meetings. But most customers were quickly in and out of the store.

This may seem counterintuitive, but keep this in mind. Slow sippers perched on poofs give a café ambience. But they are expensive customers compared to the ones who leave moments after arrival. Your best customers are the ones who show up frequently and never overstay their welcome.

Finally, the best mark of service in any coffee shop is showing your team and your customers that you are involved. Coffee is so much more than a drink. It's a diversion, a passion and a pleasure. The more you show your team that you are customer focused, the more they will follow your lead. Likewise, your customers will feel your intent. And that will make your café seem more like the place they always want to visit.

Chapter 6: The Best Plan

To this point we've focused on the fundamentals of creating a thriving coffee shop business. And using this guide you have figured out the type of café you wish to open. You've selected a location to accommodate your vision and acquired the tools necessary to produce a superior product. You understand what you are doing, how to do it well and identified the features of your shop that will make it appealing to customers. You've also figured out the way to provide superior service in addition to a top-notch product.

It's time to open the store and allow your plan to make first contact with your customers. Now you'll re-learn everything. Remember when I called your initial plan fantastic? Here is where your planning and attention to detail will yield to the reality of the market. All your assumptions will be laid to rest and you will need to adapt to reality. One of the ways to ensure that the reality of your opening meets your expectations is through the creation of brand momentum. A store with lots of activity will attract customers eager to see what it's all about. Additionally, word of mouth is the best form of marketing you can employ.

One of the best ways to capitalize on momentum is through the use of loyalty cards. Encourage frequent revisits. And more than that take a few minutes around your opening to visit local businesses and stores and give the employees some of the loyalty cards for their own use or alternately to give to their customers who look like they need a pick me up. One of the best ways to give one of these customers who walked in with a loyalty card a treat is to punch a few notches after their first trip. You've just shown them you want them back in the store. Hand them a new card and ask that they pass it along to a fellow coffee lover.

Along the same lines, promote certain products even at a loss to get people to walk in the door. Have a hump day discount where a cup of coffee is fifty cents on Wednesday afternoons because the work week is fifty percent done. A well-trained team will know that with the inexpensive coffee they should offer higher margin baked goods to balance the sale. Bundling these items together will mitigate the loss you incur on the coffee transaction. More than that it will introduce your customers to new products. Coffee is your main business. It cannot be your only business.

Finally, do not let your search for perfect pairing overwhelm your good judgment. Focus on the right compliments to your coffee offerings and not filling the menu with items that detract from the pure, simple goodness of a great cup of coffee. Even if the big chains want to compete with other quick service restaurant chains, your objective should be a singular pursuit of a great coffee experience. To do anything other than that is to betray the trust your customers place in you. They are looking for different, unique and personal. If they wanted sameness they would have walked by your store for the familiar logo of Chain Brand Coffee, Inc.

As a café proprietor, you will need to continually refresh your store. Listen to what your customers like and change the things they don't. Give them a sense of belonging and community. They will always reward you with continued patronage.

Conclusion

"Never let the perfect become the enemy of your success." Coffee shops typically provide steady and reliable earnings. That makes the owner's plan and execution of it the single biggest determinants of success. With the plan I've laid out, you are well on your way to consistent success. Before giving some final advice, let's review what we learned.

Don't be afraid to make mistakes. Instead focus on learning from the mistakes you make. With that insight you can ensure you won't make the big mistake that derails your business.

Choose a good location, but don't obsess about finding the perfect location. A good location will offer the right demographic mix, close proximity to offices, retail shops and tourist destinations.

Source superior beans from a local roaster. Acquire equipment that supports your store's focus. Heavy automation helps busy stores keep pace with customer demand.

Understand how to make the products you offer using the traditional methods as well as the fully automated standards of today. Setup the store and work areas to maximize efficiency. Make as much as you can in advance to keep the display case full during peak times.

Every visitor is an opportunity to make a customer for life. Empowering your team to make their experience memorable is one key to exceptional service. Another is taking personal involvement in your store's day to day operations.

At opening, be prepared to hustle for customers and reward them for their loyalty. Do not be afraid to relentlessly market, even through direct solicitation of new potential customers.

Thank you for purchasing this book. I sincerely hope it has enabled you to better plan to make your dreams come true. I know of no pleasure as great as building a business from startup to success. I wish you the best of luck as you seek to fulfill your dreams. If you enjoyed this book or found it helpful, I'd greatly appreciate it if you'd take a moment to leave a review on Amazon. Thank you!

Printed in Great Britain
by Amazon